The Art of War

by Sun Tzu

Translated by Lionel Giles

www.NablaBooks.com

This work is in the public domain.
Cover and interior design copyright © 2009 Nabla.

Printed in the United States of America

ISBN-13: 978-1-936276-01-1
ISBN-10: 1-936276-01-1

Contents

1 Laying Plans — 1

2 Waging War — 4

3 Attack by Stratagem — 7

4 Tactical Dispositions — 10

5 Energy — 12

6 Weak Points and Strong — 15

7 Maneuvering — 19

8 Variation in Tactics — 23

9 The Army on the March — 25

10 Terrain — 30

11 The Nine Situations — 34

12 The Attack by Fire — 41

13 The Use of Spies — 44

1. Laying Plans

1. Sun Tzu said: The art of war is of vital importance to the State.

2. It is a matter of life and death, a road either to safety or to ruin. Hence it is a subject of inquiry which can on no account be neglected.

3. The art of war, then, is governed by five constant factors, to be taken into account in one's deliberations, when seeking to determine the conditions obtaining in the field.

4. These are:

    (1) The Moral Law;

    (2) Heaven;

    (3) Earth;

    (4) The Commander;

    (5) Method and discipline.

5, 6. The Moral Law causes the people to be in complete accord with their ruler, so that they will follow him regardless of their lives, undismayed by any danger.

7. Heaven signifies night and day, cold and heat, times and seasons.

8. Earth comprises distances, great and small; danger and security; open ground and narrow passes; the chances of life and death.

9. The Commander stands for the virtues of wisdom, sincerity, benevolence, courage and strictness.

10. By method and discipline are to be understood the marshaling of the army in its proper subdivisions, the graduations of rank among the officers, the maintenance of roads by which supplies may reach the army, and the control of military expenditure.

11. These five heads should be familiar to every general: he who knows them will be victorious; he who knows them not will fail.

12. Therefore, in your deliberations, when seeking to determine the military conditions, let them be made the basis of a comparison, in this wise:–

13. (1) Which of the two sovereigns is imbued with the Moral law?
    (2) Which of the two generals has most ability?
    (3) With whom lie the advantages derived from Heaven and Earth?
    (4) On which side is discipline most rigorously enforced?
    (5) Which army is stronger?
    (6) On which side are officers and men more highly trained?
    (7) In which army is there the greater constancy both in reward and punishment?

14. By means of these seven considerations I can forecast victory or defeat.

15. The general that hearkens to my counsel and acts upon it, will conquer: let such a one be retained in command! The general that hearkens not to my counsel nor acts upon it, will suffer defeat:–let such a one be dismissed!

16. While heeding the profit of my counsel, avail yourself also of any helpful circumstances over and beyond the ordinary rules.

17. According as circumstances are favorable, one should modify one's plans.

18. All warfare is based on deception.

19. Hence, when able to attack, we must seem unable; when using our forces, we must seem inactive; when we are near, we must make the enemy believe we are far away; when far away, we must make him believe we are near.

20. Hold out baits to entice the enemy. Feign disorder, and crush him.

21. If he is secure at all points, be prepared for him. If he is in superior strength, evade him.

22. If your opponent is of choleric temper, seek to irritate him. Pretend to be weak, that he may grow arrogant.

23. If he is taking his ease, give him no rest. If his forces are united, separate them.

24. Attack him where he is unprepared, appear where you are not expected.

25. These military devices, leading to victory, must not be divulged beforehand.

26. Now the general who wins a battle makes many calculations in his temple ere the battle is fought. The general who loses a battle makes but few calculations beforehand. Thus do many calculations lead to victory, and few calculations to defeat: how much more no calculation at all! It is by attention to this point that I can foresee who is likely to win or lose.

2. Waging War

1. Sun Tzu said: In the operations of war, where there are in the field a thousand swift chariots, as many heavy chariots, and a hundred thousand mail-clad soldiers, with provisions enough to carry them a thousand mile, the expenditure at home and at the front, including entertainment of guests, small items such as glue and paint, and sums spent on chariots and armor, will reach the total of a thousand ounces of silver per day. Such is the cost of raising an army of 100,000 men.

2. When you engage in actual fighting, if victory is long in coming, then men's weapons will grow dull and their ardor will be damped. If you lay siege to a town, you will exhaust your strength.

3. Again, if the campaign is protracted, the resources of the State will not be equal to the strain.

4. Now, when your weapons are dulled, your ardor damped, your strength exhausted and your treasure spent, other chieftains will spring up to take advantage of your extremity. Then no man, however wise, will be able to avert the consequences that must ensue.

5. Thus, though we have heard of stupid haste in war, cleverness has never been seen associated with long delays.

6. There is no instance of a country having benefited from prolonged warfare.

7. It is only one who is thoroughly acquainted with the evils of war that can thoroughly understand the profitable way of carrying it on.

8. The skillful soldier does not raise a second levy, neither are his supply-wagons loaded more than twice.

9. Bring war material with you from home, but forage on the enemy. Thus the army will have food enough for its needs.

10. Poverty of the State exchequer causes an army to be maintained by contributions from a distance. Contributing to maintain an army at a distance causes the people to be impoverished.

11. On the other hand, the proximity of an army causes prices to go up; and high prices cause the people's substance to be drained away.

12. When their substance is drained away, the peasantry will be afflicted by heavy exactions.

3, 14. With this loss of substance and exhaustion of strength, the homes of the people will be stripped bare, and three-tenths of their income will be dissipated; while government expenses for broken chariots, worn-out horses, breast-plates and helmets, bows and arrows, spears and shields, protective mantles, draught-oxen and heavy wagons, will amount to four-tenths of its total revenue.

15. Hence a wise general makes a point of foraging on the enemy. One cartload of the enemy's provisions is equivalent to twenty of one's own, and likewise a single picul of his provender is equivalent to twenty from one's own store.

16. Now in order to kill the enemy, our men must be roused to anger; that there may be advantage from defeating the enemy, they must have their rewards.

17. Therefore in chariot fighting, when ten or more chariots have been taken, those should be rewarded who took the first. Our own flags should be substituted for those of the enemy, and the chariots mingled and used in conjunction with ours. The captured soldiers should be kindly treated and kept.

18. This is called, using the conquered foe to augment one's own strength.

19. In war, then, let your great object be victory, not lengthy campaigns.

20. Thus it may be known that the leader of armies is the arbiter of the people's fate, the man on whom it depends whether the nation shall be in peace or in peril.

3. Attack by Stratagem

1. Sun Tzu said: In the practical art of war, the best thing of all is to take the enemy's country whole and intact; to shatter and destroy it is not so good. So, too, it is better to recapture an army entire than to destroy it, to capture a regiment, a detachment or a company entire than to destroy them.

2. Hence to fight and conquer in all your battles is not supreme excellence; supreme excellence consists in breaking the enemy's resistance without fighting.

3. Thus the highest form of generalship is to balk the enemy's plans; the next best is to prevent the junction of the enemy's forces; the next in order is to attack the enemy's army in the field; and the worst policy of all is to besiege walled cities.

4. The rule is, not to besiege walled cities if it can possibly be avoided. The preparation of mantlets, movable shelters, and various implements of war, will take up three whole months; and the piling up of mounds over against the walls will take three months more.

5. The general, unable to control his irritation, will launch his men to the assault like swarming ants, with the result that one-third of his men are slain, while the town still remains untaken. Such are the disastrous effects of a siege.

6. Therefore the skillful leader subdues the enemy's troops without any fighting; he captures their cities without laying siege to them; he overthrows their kingdom without lengthy operations in the field.

7. With his forces intact he will dispute the mastery of the Empire, and thus, without losing a man, his triumph will be complete. This is the method of attacking by stratagem.

8. It is the rule in war, if our forces are ten to the enemy's one, to surround him; if five to one, to attack him; if twice as numerous, to divide our army into two.

9. If equally matched, we can offer battle; if slightly inferior in numbers, we can avoid the enemy; if quite unequal in every way, we can flee from him.

10. Hence, though an obstinate fight may be made by a small force, in the end it must be captured by the larger force.

11. Now the general is the bulwark of the State; if the bulwark is complete at all points; the State will be strong; if the bulwark is defective, the State will be weak.

12. There are three ways in which a ruler can bring misfortune upon his army:–

13. (1) By commanding the army to advance or to retreat, being ignorant of the fact that it cannot obey. This is called hobbling the army.

14. (2) By attempting to govern an army in the same way as he administers a kingdom, being ignorant of the conditions which obtain in an army. This causes restlessness in the soldier's minds.

15. (3) By employing the officers of his army without discrimination, through ignorance of the military principle of adaptation to circumstances. This shakes the confidence of the soldiers.

16. But when the army is restless and distrustful, trouble is sure to come from the other feudal princes. This is simply bringing anarchy into the army, and flinging victory away.

17. Thus we may know that there are five essentials for victory:

(1) He will win who knows when to fight and when not to fight.

(2) He will win who knows how to handle both superior and inferior forces.

(3) He will win whose army is animated by the same spirit throughout all its ranks.

(4) He will win who, prepared himself, waits to take the enemy unprepared.

(5) He will win who has military capacity and is not interfered with by the sovereign.

18. Hence the saying: If you know the enemy and know yourself, you need not fear the result of a hundred battles. If you know yourself but not the enemy, for every victory gained you will also suffer a defeat. If you know neither the enemy nor yourself, you will succumb in every battle.

4. Tactical Dispositions

1. Sun Tzu said: The good fighters of old first put themselves beyond the possibility of defeat, and then waited for an opportunity of defeating the enemy.

2. To secure ourselves against defeat lies in our own hands, but the opportunity of defeating the enemy is provided by the enemy himself.

3. Thus the good fighter is able to secure himself against defeat, but cannot make certain of defeating the enemy.

4. Hence the saying: One may know how to conquer without being able to do it.

5. Security against defeat implies defensive tactics; ability to defeat the enemy means taking the offensive.

6. Standing on the defensive indicates insufficient strength; attacking, a superabundance of strength.

7. The general who is skilled in defense hides in the most secret recesses of the earth; he who is skilled in attack flashes forth from the topmost heights of heaven. Thus on the one hand we have ability to protect ourselves; on the other, a victory that is complete.

8. To see victory only when it is within the ken of the common herd is not the acme of excellence.

9. Neither is it the acme of excellence if you fight and conquer and the whole Empire says, "Well done!"

10. To lift an autumn hair is no sign of great strength; to see the sun and moon is no sign of sharp sight; to hear the noise of thunder is no sign of a quick ear.

11. What the ancients called a clever fighter is one who not only wins, but excels in winning with ease.

12. Hence his victories bring him neither reputation for wisdom nor credit for courage.

13. He wins his battles by making no mistakes. Making no mistakes is what establishes the certainty of victory, for it means conquering an enemy that is already defeated.

14. Hence the skillful fighter puts himself into a position which makes defeat impossible, and does not miss the moment for defeating the enemy.

15. Thus it is that in war the victorious strategist only seeks battle after the victory has been won, whereas he who is destined to defeat first fights and afterwards looks for victory.

16. The consummate leader cultivates the moral law, and strictly adheres to method and discipline; thus it is in his power to control success.

17. In respect of military method, we have, firstly, Measurement; secondly, Estimation of quantity; thirdly, Calculation; fourthly, Balancing of chances; fifthly, Victory.

18. Measurement owes its existence to Earth; Estimation of quantity to Measurement; Calculation to Estimation of quantity; Balancing of chances to Calculation; and Victory to Balancing of chances.

19. A victorious army opposed to a routed one, is as a pound's weight placed in the scale against a single grain.

20. The onrush of a conquering force is like the bursting of pent-up waters into a chasm a thousand fathoms deep.

5. Energy

1. Sun Tzu said: The control of a large force is the same principle as the control of a few men: it is merely a question of dividing up their numbers.

2. Fighting with a large army under your command is nowise different from fighting with a small one: it is merely a question of instituting signs and signals.

3. To ensure that your whole host may withstand the brunt of the enemy's attack and remain unshaken– this is effected by maneuvers direct and indirect.

4. That the impact of your army may be like a grindstone dashed against an egg–this is effected by the science of weak points and strong.

5. In all fighting, the direct method may be used for joining battle, but indirect methods will be needed in order to secure victory.

6. Indirect tactics, efficiently applied, are inexhaustible as Heaven and Earth, unending as the flow of rivers and streams; like the sun and moon, they end but to begin anew; like the four seasons, they pass away to return once more.

7. There are not more than five musical notes, yet the combinations of these five give rise to more melodies than can ever be heard.

8. There are not more than five primary colors (blue, yellow, red, white, and black), yet in combination they produce more hues than can ever been seen.

9. There are not more than five cardinal tastes (sour, acrid, salt, sweet, bitter), yet combinations of them yield more flavors than can ever be tasted.

10. In battle, there are not more than two methods of attack—the direct and the indirect; yet these two in combination give rise to an endless series of maneuvers.

11. The direct and the indirect lead on to each other in turn. It is like moving in a circle—you never come to an end. Who can exhaust the possibilities of their combination?

12. The onset of troops is like the rush of a torrent which will even roll stones along in its course.

13. The quality of decision is like the well-timed swoop of a falcon which enables it to strike and destroy its victim.

14. Therefore the good fighter will be terrible in his onset, and prompt in his decision.

15. Energy may be likened to the bending of a crossbow; decision, to the releasing of a trigger.

16. Amid the turmoil and tumult of battle, there may be seeming disorder and yet no real disorder at all; amid confusion and chaos, your array may be without head or tail, yet it will be proof against defeat.

17. Simulated disorder postulates perfect discipline, simulated fear postulates courage; simulated weakness postulates strength.

18. Hiding order beneath the cloak of disorder is simply a question of subdivision; concealing courage under a show of timidity presupposes a fund of latent energy; masking strength with weakness is to be effected by tactical dispositions.

19. Thus one who is skillful at keeping the enemy on the move maintains deceitful appearances, according to which the enemy will act. He sacrifices something, that the enemy may snatch at it.

20. By holding out baits, he keeps him on the march; then with a body of picked men he lies in wait for him.

21. The clever combatant looks to the effect of combined energy, and does not require too much from individuals. Hence his ability to pick out the right men and utilize combined energy.

22. When he utilizes combined energy, his fighting men become as it were like unto rolling logs or stones. For it is the nature of a log or stone to remain motionless on level ground, and to move when on a slope; if four-cornered, to come to a standstill, but if round-shaped, to go rolling down.

23. Thus the energy developed by good fighting men is as the momentum of a round stone rolled down a mountain thousands of feet in height. So much on the subject of energy.

6. Weak Points and Strong

1. Sun Tzu said: Whoever is first in the field and awaits the coming of the enemy, will be fresh for the fight; whoever is second in the field and has to hasten to battle will arrive exhausted.

2. Therefore the clever combatant imposes his will on the enemy, but does not allow the enemy's will to be imposed on him.

3. By holding out advantages to him, he can cause the enemy to approach of his own accord; or, by inflicting damage, he can make it impossible for the enemy to draw near.

4. If the enemy is taking his ease, he can harass him; if well supplied with food, he can starve him out; if quietly encamped, he can force him to move.

5. Appear at points which the enemy must hasten to defend; march swiftly to places where you are not expected.

6. An army may march great distances without distress, if it marches through country where the enemy is not.

7. You can be sure of succeeding in your attacks if you only attack places which are undefended. You can ensure the safety of your defense if you only hold positions that cannot be attacked.

8. Hence that general is skillful in attack whose opponent does not know what to defend; and he is skillful in defense whose opponent does not know what to attack.

9. O divine art of subtlety and secrecy! Through you we learn to be invisible, through you inaudible; and hence we can hold the enemy's fate in our hands.

10. You may advance and be absolutely irresistible, if you make for the enemy's weak points; you may retire and be safe from pursuit if your movements are more rapid than those of the enemy.

11. If we wish to fight, the enemy can be forced to an engagement even though he be sheltered behind a high rampart and a deep ditch. All we need do is attack some other place that he will be obliged to relieve.

12. If we do not wish to fight, we can prevent the enemy from engaging us even though the lines of our encampment be merely traced out on the ground. All we need do is to throw something odd and unaccountable in his way.

13. By discovering the enemy's dispositions and remaining invisible ourselves, we can keep our forces concentrated, while the enemy's must be divided.

14. We can form a single united body, while the enemy must split up into fractions. Hence there will be a whole pitted against separate parts of a whole, which means that we shall be many to the enemy's few.

15. And if we are able thus to attack an inferior force with a superior one, our opponents will be in dire straits.

16. The spot where we intend to fight must not be made known; for then the enemy will have to prepare against a possible attack at several different points; and his forces being thus distributed in many directions, the numbers we shall have to face at any given point will be proportionately few.

17. For should the enemy strengthen his van, he will weaken his rear; should he strengthen his rear, he will weaken his van; should he strengthen his left, he will weaken his right; should he strengthen his right, he will weaken his left. If he sends reinforcements everywhere, he will everywhere be weak.

18. Numerical weakness comes from having to prepare against possible attacks; numerical strength, from compelling our adversary to make these preparations against us.

19. Knowing the place and the time of the coming battle, we may concentrate from the greatest distances in order to fight.

20. But if neither time nor place be known, then the left wing will be impotent to succor the right, the right equally impotent to succor the left, the van unable to relieve the rear, or the rear to support the van. How much more so if the furthest portions of the army are anything under a hundred LI apart, and even the nearest are separated by several LI!

21. Though according to my estimate the soldiers of Yueh exceed our own in number, that shall advantage them nothing in the matter of victory. I say then that victory can be achieved.

22. Though the enemy be stronger in numbers, we may prevent him from fighting. Scheme so as to discover his plans and the likelihood of their success.

23. Rouse him, and learn the principle of his activity or inactivity. Force him to reveal himself, so as to find out his vulnerable spots.

24. Carefully compare the opposing army with your own, so that you may know where strength is superabundant and where it is deficient.

25. In making tactical dispositions, the highest pitch you can attain is to conceal them; conceal your dispositions, and you will be safe from the prying of the subtlest spies, from the machinations of the wisest brains.

26. How victory may be produced for them out of the enemy's own tactics–that is what the multitude cannot comprehend.

27. All men can see the tactics whereby I conquer, but what none can see is the strategy out of which victory is evolved.

28. Do not repeat the tactics which have gained you one victory, but let your methods be regulated by the infinite variety of circumstances.

29. Military tactics are like unto water; for water in its natural course runs away from high places and hastens downwards.

30. So in war, the way is to avoid what is strong and to strike at what is weak.

31. Water shapes its course according to the nature of the ground over which it flows; the soldier works out his victory in relation to the foe whom he is facing.

32. Therefore, just as water retains no constant shape, so in warfare there are no constant conditions.

33. He who can modify his tactics in relation to his opponent and thereby succeed in winning, may be called a heaven-born captain.

34. The five elements (water, fire, wood, metal, earth) are not always equally predominant; the four seasons make way for each other in turn. There are short days and long; the moon has its periods of waning and waxing.

7. Maneuvering

1. Sun Tzu said: In war, the general receives his commands from the sovereign.

2. Having collected an army and concentrated his forces, he must blend and harmonize the different elements thereof before pitching his camp.

3. After that, comes tactical maneuvering, than which there is nothing more difficult. The difficulty of tactical maneuvering consists in turning the devious into the direct, and misfortune into gain.

4. Thus, to take a long and circuitous route, after enticing the enemy out of the way, and though starting after him, to contrive to reach the goal before him, shows knowledge of the artifice of DEVIATION.

5. Maneuvering with an army is advantageous; with an undisciplined multitude, most dangerous.

6. If you set a fully equipped army in march in order to snatch an advantage, the chances are that you will be too late. On the other hand, to detach a flying column for the purpose involves the sacrifice of its baggage and stores.

7. Thus, if you order your men to roll up their buff-coats, and make forced marches without halting day or night, covering double the usual distance at a stretch, doing a hundred LI in order to wrest an advantage, the leaders of all your three divisions will fall into the hands of the enemy.

8. The stronger men will be in front, the jaded ones will fall behind, and on this plan only one-tenth of your army will reach its destination.

9. If you march fifty LI in order to outmaneuver the enemy, you will lose the leader of your first division, and only half your force will reach the goal.

10. If you march thirty LI with the same object, two-thirds of your army will arrive.

11. We may take it then that an army without its baggage-train is lost; without provisions it is lost; without bases of supply it is lost.

12. We cannot enter into alliances until we are acquainted with the designs of our neighbors.

13. We are not fit to lead an army on the march unless we are familiar with the face of the country–its mountains and forests, its pitfalls and precipices, its marshes and swamps.

14. We shall be unable to turn natural advantage to account unless we make use of local guides.

15. In war, practice dissimulation, and you will succeed.

16. Whether to concentrate or to divide your troops, must be decided by circumstances.

17. Let your rapidity be that of the wind, your compactness that of the forest.

18. In raiding and plundering be like fire, is immovability like a mountain.

19. Let your plans be dark and impenetrable as night, and when you move, fall like a thunderbolt.

20. When you plunder a countryside, let the spoil be divided amongst your men; when you capture new territory, cut it up into allotments for the benefit of the soldiery.

21. Ponder and deliberate before you make a move.

22. He will conquer who has learnt the artifice of deviation. Such is the art of maneuvering.

23. The Book of Army Management says: On the field of battle, the spoken word does not carry far enough: hence the institution of gongs and drums. Nor can ordinary objects be seen clearly enough: hence the institution of banners and flags.

24. Gongs and drums, banners and flags, are means whereby the ears and eyes of the host may be focused on one particular point.

25. The host thus forming a single united body, is it impossible either for the brave to advance alone, or for the cowardly to retreat alone. This is the art of handling large masses of men.

26. In night-fighting, then, make much use of signal-fires and drums, and in fighting by day, of flags and banners, as a means of influencing the ears and eyes of your army.

27. A whole army may be robbed of its spirit; a commander-in-chief may be robbed of his presence of mind.

28. Now a soldier's spirit is keenest in the morning; by noonday it has begun to flag; and in the evening, his mind is bent only on returning to camp.

29. A clever general, therefore, avoids an army when its spirit is keen, but attacks it when it is sluggish and inclined to return. This is the art of studying moods.

30. Disciplined and calm, to await the appearance of disorder and hubbub amongst the enemy:–this is the art of retaining self-possession

31. To be near the goal while the enemy is still far from it, to wait at ease while the enemy is toiling and struggling, to be well-fed while the enemy is famished:–this is the art of husbanding one's strength.

32. To refrain from intercepting an enemy whose banners are in perfect order, to refrain from attacking an army drawn up in calm and confident array:–this is the art of studying circumstances.

33. It is a military axiom not to advance uphill against the enemy, nor to oppose him when he comes downhill.

34. Do not pursue an enemy who simulates flight; do not attack soldiers whose temper is keen.

35. Do not swallow bait offered by the enemy. Do not interfere with an army that is returning home.

36. When you surround an army, leave an outlet free. Do not press a desperate foe too hard.

37. Such is the art of warfare.

8. Variation in Tactics

1. Sun Tzu said: In war, the general receives his commands from the sovereign, collects his army and concentrates his forces

2. When in difficult country, do not encamp. In country where high roads intersect, join hands with your allies. Do not linger in dangerously isolated positions. In hemmed-in situations, you must resort to stratagem. In desperate position, you must fight.

3. There are roads which must not be followed, armies which must be not attacked, towns which must not be besieged, positions which must not be contested, commands of the sovereign which must not be obeyed.

4. The general who thoroughly understands the advantages that accompany variation of tactics knows how to handle his troops.

5. The general who does not understand these, may be well acquainted with the configuration of the country, yet he will not be able to turn his knowledge to practical account.

6. So, the student of war who is unversed in the art of war of varying his plans, even though he be acquainted with the Five Advantages, will fail to make the best use of his men.

7. Hence in the wise leader's plans, considerations of advantage and of disadvantage will be blended together.

8. If our expectation of advantage be tempered in this way, we may succeed in accomplishing the essential part of our schemes.

9. If, on the other hand, in the midst of difficulties we are always ready to seize an advantage, we may extricate ourselves from misfortune.

10. Reduce the hostile chiefs by inflicting damage on them; and make trouble for them, and keep them constantly engaged; hold out specious allurements, and make them rush to any given point.

11. The art of war teaches us to rely not on the likelihood of the enemy's not coming, but on our own readiness to receive him; not on the chance of his not attacking, but rather on the fact that we have made our position unassailable.

12. There are five dangerous faults which may affect a general:

    (1) Recklessness, which leads to destruction;
    (2) cowardice, which leads to capture;
    (3) a hasty temper, which can be provoked by insults;
    (4) a delicacy of honor which is sensitive to shame;
    (5) over-solicitude for his men, which exposes him to worry and trouble.

13. These are the five besetting sins of a general, ruinous to the conduct of war.

14. When an army is overthrown and its leader slain, the cause will surely be found among these five dangerous faults. Let them be a subject of meditation.

9. The Army on the March

1. Sun Tzu said: We come now to the question of encamping the army, and observing signs of the enemy. Pass quickly over mountains, and keep in the neighborhood of valleys.

2. Camp in high places, facing the sun. Do not climb heights in order to fight. So much for mountain warfare.

3. After crossing a river, you should get far away from it.

4. When an invading force crosses a river in its onward march, do not advance to meet it in mid-stream. It will be best to let half the army get across, and then deliver your attack.

5. If you are anxious to fight, you should not go to meet the invader near a river which he has to cross.

6. Moor your craft higher up than the enemy, and facing the sun. Do not move up-stream to meet the enemy. So much for river warfare.

7. In crossing salt-marshes, your sole concern should be to get over them quickly, without any delay.

8. If forced to fight in a salt-marsh, you should have water and grass near you, and get your back to a clump of trees. So much for operations in salt-marches.

9. In dry, level country, take up an easily accessible position with rising ground to your right and on your rear, so that the danger may be in front, and safety lie behind. So much for campaigning in flat country.

10. These are the four useful branches of military knowledge which enabled the Yellow Emperor to vanquish four several sovereigns.

11. All armies prefer high ground to low and sunny places to dark.

12. If you are careful of your men, and camp on hard ground, the army will be free from disease of every kind, and this will spell victory.

13. When you come to a hill or a bank, occupy the sunny side, with the slope on your right rear. Thus you will at once act for the benefit of your soldiers and utilize the natural advantages of the ground.

14. When, in consequence of heavy rains up-country, a river which you wish to ford is swollen and flecked with foam, you must wait until it subsides.

15. Country in which there are precipitous cliffs with torrents running between, deep natural hollows, confined places, tangled thickets, quagmires and crevasses, should be left with all possible speed and not approached.

16. While we keep away from such places, we should get the enemy to approach them; while we face them, we should let the enemy have them on his rear.

17. If in the neighborhood of your camp there should be any hilly country, ponds surrounded by aquatic grass, hollow basins filled with reeds, or woods with thick undergrowth, they must be carefully routed out and searched; for these are places where men in ambush or insidious spies are likely to be lurking.

18. When the enemy is close at hand and remains quiet, he is relying on the natural strength of his position.

19. When he keeps aloof and tries to provoke a battle, he is anxious for the other side to advance.

20. If his place of encampment is easy of access, he is tendering a bait.

21. Movement amongst the trees of a forest shows that the enemy is advancing. The appearance of a number of screens in the midst of thick grass means that the enemy wants to make us suspicious.

22. The rising of birds in their flight is the sign of an ambuscade. Startled beasts indicate that a sudden attack is coming.

23. When there is dust rising in a high column, it is the sign of chariots advancing; when the dust is low, but spread over a wide area, it betokens the approach of infantry. When it branches out in different directions, it shows that parties have been sent to collect firewood. A few clouds of dust moving to and fro signify that the army is encamping.

24. Humble words and increased preparations are signs that the enemy is about to advance. Violent language and driving forward as if to the attack are signs that he will retreat.

25. When the light chariots come out first and take up a position on the wings, it is a sign that the enemy is forming for battle.

26. Peace proposals unaccompanied by a sworn covenant indicate a plot.

27. When there is much running about and the soldiers fall into rank, it means that the critical moment has come.

28. When some are seen advancing and some retreating, it is a lure.

29. When the soldiers stand leaning on their spears, they are faint from want of food.

30. If those who are sent to draw water begin by drinking themselves, the army is suffering from thirst.

31. If the enemy sees an advantage to be gained and makes no effort to secure it, the soldiers are exhausted.

32. If birds gather on any spot, it is unoccupied. Clamor by night betokens nervousness.

33. If there is disturbance in the camp, the general's authority is weak. If the banners and flags are shifted about, sedition is afoot. If the officers are angry, it means that the men are weary.

34. When an army feeds its horses with grain and kills its cattle for food, and when the men do not hang their cooking-pots over the camp-fires, showing that they will not return to their tents, you may know that they are determined to fight to the death.

35. The sight of men whispering together in small knots or speaking in subdued tones points to disaffection amongst the rank and file.

36. Too frequent rewards signify that the enemy is at the end of his resources; too many punishments betray a condition of dire distress.

37. To begin by bluster, but afterwards to take fright at the enemy's numbers, shows a supreme lack of intelligence.

38. When envoys are sent with compliments in their mouths, it is a sign that the enemy wishes for a truce.

39. If the enemy's troops march up angrily and remain facing ours for a long time without either joining battle or taking themselves off again, the situation is one that demands great vigilance and circumspection.

40. If our troops are no more in number than the enemy, that is amply sufficient; it only means that no direct attack can be made. What we can do is simply to concentrate all our available strength, keep a close watch on the enemy, and obtain reinforcements.

41. He who exercises no forethought but makes light of his opponents is sure to be captured by them.

42. If soldiers are punished before they have grown attached to you, they will not prove submissive; and, unless submissive, then will be practically useless. If, when the soldiers have become

attached to you, punishments are not enforced, they will still be useless.

43. Therefore soldiers must be treated in the first instance with humanity, but kept under control by means of iron discipline. This is a certain road to victory.

44. If in training soldiers commands are habitually enforced, the army will be well-disciplined; if not, its discipline will be bad.

45. If a general shows confidence in his men but always insists on his orders being obeyed, the gain will be mutual.

10. Terrain

1. Sun Tzu said: We may distinguish six kinds of terrain, to wit:

    (1) Accessible ground;

    (2) entangling ground;

    (3) temporizing ground;

    (4) narrow passes;

    (5) precipitous heights;

    (6) positions at a great distance from the enemy.

2. Ground which can be freely traversed by both sides is called accessible.

3. With regard to ground of this nature, be before the enemy in occupying the raised and sunny spots, and carefully guard your line of supplies. Then you will be able to fight with advantage.

4. Ground which can be abandoned but is hard to re-occupy is called entangling.

5. From a position of this sort, if the enemy is unprepared, you may sally forth and defeat him. But if the enemy is prepared for your coming, and you fail to defeat him, then, return being impossible, disaster will ensue.

6. When the position is such that neither side will gain by making the first move, it is called temporizing ground.

7. In a position of this sort, even though the enemy should offer us an attractive bait, it will be advisable not to stir forth, but rather to retreat, thus enticing the enemy in his turn; then, when part of his army has come out, we may deliver our attack with advantage.

8. With regard to narrow passes, if you can occupy them first, let them be strongly garrisoned and await the advent of the enemy.

9. Should the army forestall you in occupying a pass, do not go after him if the pass is fully garrisoned, but only if it is weakly garrisoned.

10. With regard to precipitous heights, if you are beforehand with your adversary, you should occupy the raised and sunny spots, and there wait for him to come up.

11. If the enemy has occupied them before you, do not follow him, but retreat and try to entice him away.

12. If you are situated at a great distance from the enemy, and the strength of the two armies is equal, it is not easy to provoke a battle, and fighting will be to your disadvantage.

13. These six are the principles connected with Earth. The general who has attained a responsible post must be careful to study them.

14. Now an army is exposed to six several calamities, not arising from natural causes, but from faults for which the general is responsible. These are:

    (1) Flight;
    (2) insubordination;
    (3) collapse;
    (4) ruin;
    (5) disorganization;
    (6) rout.

15. Other conditions being equal, if one force is hurled against another ten times its size, the result will be the flight of the former.

16. When the common soldiers are too strong and their officers too weak, the result is insubordination. When the officers are too strong and the common soldiers too weak, the result is collapse.

17. When the higher officers are angry and insubordinate, and on meeting the enemy give battle on their own account from a feeling of resentment, before the commander-in-chief can tell whether or not he is in a position to fight, the result is ruin.

18. When the general is weak and without authority; when his orders are not clear and distinct; when there are no fixes duties assigned to officers and men, and the ranks are formed in a slovenly haphazard manner, the result is utter disorganization.

19. When a general, unable to estimate the enemy's strength, allows an inferior force to engage a larger one, or hurls a weak detachment against a powerful one, and neglects to place picked soldiers in the front rank, the result must be rout.

20. These are six ways of courting defeat, which must be carefully noted by the general who has attained a responsible post.

21. The natural formation of the country is the soldier's best ally; but a power of estimating the adversary, of controlling the forces of victory, and of shrewdly calculating difficulties, dangers and distances, constitutes the test of a great general.

22. He who knows these things, and in fighting puts his knowledge into practice, will win his battles. He who knows them not, nor practices them, will surely be defeated.

23. If fighting is sure to result in victory, then you must fight, even though the ruler forbid it; if fighting will not result in victory, then you must not fight even at the ruler's bidding.

24. The general who advances without coveting fame and retreats without fearing disgrace, whose only thought is to protect his country and do good service for his sovereign, is the jewel of the kingdom.

25. Regard your soldiers as your children, and they will follow you into the deepest valleys; look upon them as your own beloved sons, and they will stand by you even unto death.

26. If, however, you are indulgent, but unable to make your authority felt; kind-hearted, but unable to enforce your commands; and incapable, moreover, of quelling disorder: then your soldiers must be likened to spoilt children; they are useless for any practical purpose.

27. If we know that our own men are in a condition to attack, but are unaware that the enemy is not open to attack, we have gone only halfway towards victory.

28. If we know that the enemy is open to attack, but are unaware that our own men are not in a condition to attack, we have gone only halfway towards victory.

29. If we know that the enemy is open to attack, and also know that our men are in a condition to attack, but are unaware that the nature of the ground makes fighting impracticable, we have still gone only halfway towards victory.

30. Hence the experienced soldier, once in motion, is never bewildered; once he has broken camp, he is never at a loss.

31. Hence the saying: If you know the enemy and know yourself, your victory will not stand in doubt; if you know Heaven and know Earth, you may make your victory complete.

11. The Nine Situations

1. Sun Tzu said that the art of war recognizes nine varieties of ground:

    (1) Dispersive ground;

    (2) facile ground;

    (3) contentious ground;

    (4) open ground;

    (5) ground of intersecting highways;

    (6) serious ground;

    (7) difficult ground;

    (8) hemmed-in ground;

    (9) desperate ground.

2. When a chieftain is fighting in his own territory, it is dispersive ground.

3. When he has penetrated into hostile territory, but to no great distance, it is facile ground.

4. Ground the possession of which imports great advantage to either side, is contentious ground.

5. Ground on which each side has liberty of movement is open ground.

6. Ground which forms the key to three contiguous states, so that he who occupies it first has most of the Empire at his command, is a ground of intersecting highways.

7. When an army has penetrated into the heart of a hostile country, leaving a number of fortified cities in its rear, it is serious ground.

8. Mountain forests, rugged steeps, marshes and fens–all country that is hard to traverse: this is difficult ground.

9. Ground which is reached through narrow gorges, and from which we can only retire by tortuous paths, so that a small number of the enemy would suffice to crush a large body of our men: this is hemmed in ground.

10. Ground on which we can only be saved from destruction by fighting without delay, is desperate ground.

11. On dispersive ground, therefore, fight not. On facile ground, halt not. On contentious ground, attack not.

12. On open ground, do not try to block the enemy's way. On the ground of intersecting highways, join hands with your allies.

13. On serious ground, gather in plunder. In difficult ground, keep steadily on the march.

14. On hemmed-in ground, resort to stratagem. On desperate ground, fight.

15. Those who were called skillful leaders of old knew how to drive a wedge between the enemy's front and rear; to prevent co-operation between his large and small divisions; to hinder the good troops from rescuing the bad, the officers from rallying their men.

16. When the enemy's men were united, they managed to keep them in disorder.

17. When it was to their advantage, they made a forward move; when otherwise, they stopped still.

18. If asked how to cope with a great host of the enemy in orderly array and on the point of marching to the attack, I should say: "Begin by seizing something which your opponent holds dear; then he will be amenable to your will."

19. Rapidity is the essence of war: take advantage of the enemy's unreadiness, make your way by unexpected routes, and attack unguarded spots.

20. The following are the principles to be observed by an invading force: The further you penetrate into a country, the greater will be the solidarity of your troops, and thus the defenders will not prevail against you.

21. Make forays in fertile country in order to supply your army with food.

22. Carefully study the well-being of your men, and do not overtax them. Concentrate your energy and hoard your strength. Keep your army continually on the move, and devise unfathomable plans.

23. Throw your soldiers into positions whence there is no escape, and they will prefer death to flight. If they will face death, there is nothing they may not achieve. Officers and men alike will put forth their uttermost strength.

24. Soldiers when in desperate straits lose the sense of fear. If there is no place of refuge, they will stand firm. If they are in hostile country, they will show a stubborn front. If there is no help for it, they will fight hard.

25. Thus, without waiting to be marshaled, the soldiers will be constantly on the qui vive; without waiting to be asked, they will do your will; without restrictions, they will be faithful; without giving orders, they can be trusted.

26. Prohibit the taking of omens, and do away with superstitious doubts. Then, until death itself comes, no calamity need be feared.

27. If our soldiers are not overburdened with money, it is not because they have a distaste for riches; if their lives are not unduly long, it is not because they are disinclined to longevity.

28. On the day they are ordered out to battle, your soldiers may weep, those sitting up bedewing their garments, and those lying down letting the tears run down their cheeks. But let them once be brought to bay, and they will display the courage of a Chu or a Kuei.

29. The skillful tactician may be likened to the shuai-jan. Now the shuai-jan is a snake that is found in the ChUng mountains. Strike at its head, and you will be attacked by its tail; strike at its tail, and you will be attacked by its head; strike at its middle, and you will be attacked by head and tail both.

30. Asked if an army can be made to imitate the shuai-jan, I should answer, Yes. For the men of Wu and the men of Yueh are enemies; yet if they are crossing a river in the same boat and are caught by a storm, they will come to each other's assistance just as the left hand helps the right.

31. Hence it is not enough to put one's trust in the tethering of horses, and the burying of chariot wheels in the ground

32. The principle on which to manage an army is to set up one standard of courage which all must reach.

33. How to make the best of both strong and weak–that is a question involving the proper use of ground.

34. Thus the skillful general conducts his army just as though he were leading a single man, willy-nilly, by the hand.

35. It is the business of a general to be quiet and thus ensure secrecy; upright and just, and thus maintain order.

36. He must be able to mystify his officers and men by false reports and appearances, and thus keep them in total ignorance.

37. By altering his arrangements and changing his plans, he keeps the enemy without definite knowledge. By shifting his camp and taking circuitous routes, he prevents the enemy from anticipating his purpose.

38. At the critical moment, the leader of an army acts like one who has climbed up a height and then kicks away the ladder behind him. He carries his men deep into hostile territory before he shows his hand.

39. He burns his boats and breaks his cooking-pots; like a shepherd driving a flock of sheep, he drives his men this way and that, and nothing knows whither he is going.

40. To muster his host and bring it into danger:–this may be termed the business of the general.

41. The different measures suited to the nine varieties of ground; the expediency of aggressive or defensive tactics; and the fundamental laws of human nature: these are things that must most certainly be studied.

42. When invading hostile territory, the general principle is, that penetrating deeply brings cohesion; penetrating but a short way means dispersion.

43. When you leave your own country behind, and take your army across neighborhood territory, you find yourself on critical ground. When there are means of communication on all four sides, the ground is one of intersecting highways.

44. When you penetrate deeply into a country, it is serious ground. When you penetrate but a little way, it is facile ground.

45. When you have the enemy's strongholds on your rear, and narrow passes in front, it is hemmed-in ground. When there is no place of refuge at all, it is desperate ground.

46. Therefore, on dispersive ground, I would inspire my men with unity of purpose. On facile ground, I would see that there is close connection between all parts of my army.

47. On contentious ground, I would hurry up my rear.

48. On open ground, I would keep a vigilant eye on my defenses. On ground of intersecting highways, I would consolidate my alliances.

49. On serious ground, I would try to ensure a continuous stream of supplies. On difficult ground, I would keep pushing on along the road.

50. On hemmed-in ground, I would block any way of retreat. On desperate ground, I would proclaim to my soldiers the hopelessness of saving their lives.

51. For it is the soldier's disposition to offer an obstinate resistance when surrounded, to fight hard when he cannot help himself, and to obey promptly when he has fallen into danger.

52. We cannot enter into alliance with neighboring princes until we are acquainted with their designs. We are not fit to lead an army on the march unless we are familiar with the face of the country–its mountains and forests, its pitfalls and precipices, its marshes and swamps. We shall be unable to turn natural advantages to account unless we make use of local guides.

53. To be ignored of any one of the following four or five principles does not befit a warlike prince.

54. When a warlike prince attacks a powerful state, his generalship shows itself in preventing the concentration of the enemy's forces. He overawes his opponents, and their allies are prevented from joining against him.

55. Hence he does not strive to ally himself with all and sundry, nor does he foster the power of other states. He carries out his own secret designs, keeping his antagonists in awe. Thus he is able to capture their cities and overthrow their kingdoms.

56. Bestow rewards without regard to rule, issue orders without regard to previous arrangements; and you will be able to handle a whole army as though you had to do with but a single man.

57. Confront your soldiers with the deed itself; never let them know your design. When the outlook is bright, bring it before their eyes; but tell them nothing when the situation is gloomy.

58. Place your army in deadly peril, and it will survive; plunge it into desperate straits, and it will come off in safety.

59. For it is precisely when a force has fallen into harm's way that is capable of striking a blow for victory.

60. Success in warfare is gained by carefully accommodating ourselves to the enemy's purpose.

61. By persistently hanging on the enemy's flank, we shall succeed in the long run in killing the commander-in-chief.

62. This is called ability to accomplish a thing by sheer cunning.

63. On the day that you take up your command, block the frontier passes, destroy the official tallies, and stop the passage of all emissaries.

64. Be stern in the council-chamber, so that you may control the situation.

65. If the enemy leaves a door open, you must rush in.

66. Forestall your opponent by seizing what he holds dear, and subtly contrive to time his arrival on the ground.

67. Walk in the path defined by rule, and accommodate yourself to the enemy until you can fight a decisive battle.

68. At first, then, exhibit the coyness of a maiden, until the enemy gives you an opening; afterwards emulate the rapidity of a running hare, and it will be too late for the enemy to oppose you.

12. The Attack by Fire

1. Sun Tzu said: There are five ways of attacking with fire. The first is to burn soldiers in their camp; the second is to burn stores; the third is to burn baggage trains; the fourth is to burn arsenals and magazines; the fifth is to hurl dropping fire amongst the enemy.

2. In order to carry out an attack, we must have means available. The material for raising fire should always be kept in readiness.

3. There is a proper season for making attacks with fire, and special days for starting a conflagration.

4. The proper season is when the weather is very dry; the special days are those when the moon is in the constellations of the Sieve, the Wall, the Wing or the Cross-bar; for these four are all days of rising wind.

5. In attacking with fire, one should be prepared to meet five possible developments:

6. (1) When fire breaks out inside the enemy's camp, respond at once with an attack from without.

7. (2) If there is an outbreak of fire, but the enemy's soldiers remain quiet, bide your time and do not attack.

8. (3) When the force of the flames has reached its height, follow it up with an attack, if that is practicable; if not, stay where you are.

9. (4) If it is possible to make an assault with fire from without, do not wait for it to break out within, but deliver your attack at a favorable moment.

10. (5) When you start a fire, be to windward of it. Do not attack from the leeward.

11. A wind that rises in the daytime lasts long, but a night breeze soon falls.

12. In every army, the five developments connected with fire must be known, the movements of the stars calculated, and a watch kept for the proper days.

13. Hence those who use fire as an aid to the attack show intelligence; those who use water as an aid to the attack gain an accession of strength.

14. By means of water, an enemy may be intercepted, but not robbed of all his belongings.

15. Unhappy is the fate of one who tries to win his battles and succeed in his attacks without cultivating the spirit of enterprise; for the result is waste of time and general stagnation.

16. Hence the saying: The enlightened ruler lays his plans well ahead; the good general cultivates his resources.

17. Move not unless you see an advantage; use not your troops unless there is something to be gained; fight not unless the position is critical.

18. No ruler should put troops into the field merely to gratify his own spleen; no general should fight a battle simply out of pique.

19. If it is to your advantage, make a forward move; if not, stay where you are.

20. Anger may in time change to gladness; vexation may be succeeded by content.

21. But a kingdom that has once been destroyed can never come again into being; nor can the dead ever be brought back to life.

22. Hence the enlightened ruler is heedful, and the good general full of caution. This is the way to keep a country at peace and an army intact.

13. The Use of Spies

1. Sun Tzu said: Raising a host of a hundred thousand men and marching them great distances entails heavy loss on the people and a drain on the resources of the State. The daily expenditure will amount to a thousand ounces of silver. There will be commotion at home and abroad, and men will drop down exhausted on the highways. As many as seven hundred thousand families will be impeded in their labor.

2. Hostile armies may face each other for years, striving for the victory which is decided in a single day. This being so, to remain in ignorance of the enemy's condition simply because one grudges the outlay of a hundred ounces of silver in honors and emoluments, is the height of inhumanity.

3. One who acts thus is no leader of men, no present help to his sovereign, no master of victory.

4. Thus, what enables the wise sovereign and the good general to strike and conquer, and achieve things beyond the reach of ordinary men, is foreknowledge.

5. Now this foreknowledge cannot be elicited from spirits; it cannot be obtained inductively from experience, nor by any deductive calculation.

6. Knowledge of the enemy's dispositions can only be obtained from other men.

7. Hence the use of spies, of whom there are five classes:

    (1) Local spies;

    (2) inward spies;

(3) converted spies;

(4) doomed spies;

(5) surviving spies.

8. When these five kinds of spy are all at work, none can discover the secret system. This is called "divine manipulation of the threads." It is the sovereign's most precious faculty.

9. Having local spies means employing the services of the inhabitants of a district.

10. Having inward spies, making use of officials of the enemy.

11. Having converted spies, getting hold of the enemy's spies and using them for our own purposes.

12. Having doomed spies, doing certain things openly for purposes of deception, and allowing our spies to know of them and report them to the enemy.

13. Surviving spies, finally, are those who bring back news from the enemy's camp.

14. Hence it is that which none in the whole army are more intimate relations to be maintained than with spies. None should be more liberally rewarded. In no other business should greater secrecy be preserved.

15. Spies cannot be usefully employed without a certain intuitive sagacity.

16. They cannot be properly managed without benevolence and straightforwardness.

17. Without subtle ingenuity of mind, one cannot make certain of the truth of their reports.

18. Be subtle! be subtle! and use your spies for every kind of business.

19. If a secret piece of news is divulged by a spy before the time is ripe, he must be put to death together with the man to whom the secret was told.

20. Whether the object be to crush an army, to storm a city, or to assassinate an individual, it is always necessary to begin by finding out the names of the attendants, the aides-de-camp, and doorkeepers and sentries of the general in command. Our spies must be commissioned to ascertain these.

21. The enemy's spies who have come to spy on us must be sought out, tempted with bribes, led away and comfortably housed. Thus they will become converted spies and available for our service.

22. It is through the information brought by the converted spy that we are able to acquire and employ local and inward spies.

23. It is owing to his information, again, that we can cause the doomed spy to carry false tidings to the enemy.

24. Lastly, it is by his information that the surviving spy can be used on appointed occasions.

25. The end and aim of spying in all its five varieties is knowledge of the enemy; and this knowledge can only be derived, in the first instance, from the converted spy. Hence it is essential that the converted spy be treated with the utmost liberality.

26. Of old, the rise of the Yin dynasty was due to I Chih who had served under the Hsia. Likewise, the rise of the Chou dynasty was due to Lu Ya who had served under the Yin.

27. Hence it is only the enlightened ruler and the wise general who will use the highest intelligence of the army for purposes of spying and thereby they achieve great results. Spies are a most important element in war, because on them depends an army's ability to move.

CPSIA information can be obtained at www.ICGtesting.com
Printed in the USA
LVOW06s1937101213

364719LV00001B/100/P

Hurry Up and Slow Down— Laura's Story

Laura Ferreira

Order this book online at www.trafford.com
or email orders@trafford.com

Most Trafford titles are also available at major online book retailers.

© Copyright 2012 Laura Ferreira.

All rights reserved. No part of this publication may be reproduced, stored in a retrieval system, or transmitted, in any form or by any means, electronic, mechanical, photocopying, recording, or otherwise, without the written prior permission of the author.

Printed in the United States of America.

ISBN: 978-1-4669-3692-8 (sc)
ISBN: 978-1-4669-3694-2 (hc)
ISBN: 978-1-4669-3693-5 (e)

Library of Congress Control Number: 2012909912

Trafford rev. 07/12/2012

 www.trafford.com

North America & international
toll-free: 1 888 232 4444 (USA & Canada)
phone: 250 383 6864 ♦ fax: 812 355 4082

Dedication

I dedicate this book in loving memory of my father, Jose Bothelo Feijo; my mother, Maria Deodata Feijo; my loving husband, Joe Ferreira; and our sons Jason and James Ferreira.

Hurry Up and Slow Down—Laura's Story

I have always had this burning desire to be an investigative journalist, but it would have meant quitting a well-paying job and going back to school. I was too chicken to make the change, and I have regretted it. Fortunately, I was in a job as an HR case manager, which meant that I investigated employee issues and concerns. This job allowed me to apply an investigative approach. In a way, I fulfilled my interest by gathering facts and writing my findings and recommendations in a formal report, which allowed me to apply my writing skills. In my mind, I became a pseudo investigative journalist. The point I want to make here is that if you have burning desires but can't make the change, find a creative way to fulfill them.

I also had a goal of writing a book some day and planned that for my retirement years. With the horrific year in 2010 when I came so close to death, I decided that now is as good a time as any to write it. My book is about how we are all caught up in the rat race of life, which got me thinking about the story of the tortoise and the hare and remembering it was the tortoise who won the race. Sure, the tortoise was slow, but he was steady. That's why I entitled my book *Hurry Up and Slow Down*. Slow down! I suggest you do that now, now while you can, since you can't turn back or create more time.

We've all heard the expression "Life is too short," and man, is that ever true. It's not just a cliché! I want to share with you my true life story and the catastrophic events my family and I have endured, how we have overcome these adversities, and what I have personally learned along the way. I want to share my life lessons so that you might reflect and focus on your life. Hopefully, my life lessons will help you to make changes in your life to make it more fulfilling and enjoyable.

First, let me tell you a little bit about myself and my family. I come from a Portuguese background. My parents were born in São Miguel, one of the nine islands surrounding Portugal that make up the Azores. My parents came to Canada with nothing but the clothes on their backs in the hopes of starting a new and better life. They settled in a house in the Kensington Market area, which they shared with my godparents and their two sons. If you are not familiar with Toronto, Kensington Market is now a unique, eclectic, popular market within a very diverse neighborhood. It is a popular shopping spot for locals to pick up herbs, fresh fruits, and vegetables from around the world.

When I lived there as a kid, it was a very dirty and smelly neighborhood because there were live chickens for sale on the sidewalk and fresh fish on ice outside the storefronts of the fish markets. We grew up as a very poor family.

Hurry Up and Slow Down—Laura's Story

Shortly after moving to Canada, my parents started their family, and in January 1959, my twin sister, Anjos, and I were born. In June 1960, my brother Gilbert and his twin, Liz, were born, and in August 1961, our baby sister, Mary Jo, was born. So in a span of three years, our parents had five kids. Clearly, my parents were good Catholics who didn't practice birth control.

My father was a construction worker. His work was seasonal, and so he was often out of work, although construction paid reasonably well when he was working. While unemployed, my father would help around the house by doing laundry, buying groceries, and preparing meals. My father was the sweetest, kindest man I have ever known in my life, unlike the stereotypical European fathers who tend to be very stern and strict. As a little girl, I remember sitting on the front steps, waiting for him to come home from work. As he would approach our home, I'd see him carrying his silver-aluminum lunch pail in his hand. When he would reach me, he'd kiss and hug me, and he would open up his lunch pail and say, "I brought you home a honey bun because you are my sweet honey bun." He made me feel so loved and special. It was our little secret that we shared so my siblings wouldn't get jealous. He'd also buy Life Savers candies and hide one roll in his hand, holding it tightly closed, and all five of us kids would play a game with him where we had to guess the hand that the candy was in. The one who guessed correctly got the candy.

My mother needed to work outside the home to help pay for the essentials of life (food and housing). So at the age of eight, I took on the responsibility of walking my brother and sisters to and from school every day. I learned about responsibility very early in my life. That became the core of my being—Laura, always the mature and responsible one! That was me!

My mother worked in a poultry factory plucking feathers. This was a low-paying job in a very dismal and unhealthy environment. She worked long hours and weekends. Even though she was thoroughly exhausted from having been on her feet all day, she still had a smile on her face. When she got home from work, she was happy to see us all safe and sound. Her strong work ethic caused her boss to tell her once again that she was his best worker. She took pride in her work and liked the recognition. She would seem to beam as she would tell us about her day. My mother was the disciplinarian parent—small at five-foot nothing but very mighty. I never wanted to cross my mother or cause her to be upset with me. I knew she was the boss of our house!

I had a real-life bogeyman who taught me fear. What is fear anyway? Fear is the unknown and comes from ignorance of the unknown. I didn't know this person, but his appearance scared me. I will never forget the first time I saw him. He was in the park, filling his shoe with water from the fountain. Then he drank the water from his shoe. He was a homeless person with a massive chin, bigger than Brian Mulroney's, and that's how my siblings and I identified him—"the man with the big chin." This was when I learned fear of the unknown and unfamiliar. Now I realize I was being judgmental, but heck, I was just a kid! However, prejudices do form at an early age. One day, my twin played a terrible trick on me. She told me that she had to show me a new bubblegum in the machine, and when we turned the corner, there was my bogeyman. I was so scared I shit my pants and ran home crying all the way. Kids can be so cruel. To this day, I still hold this prank against my twin sister, Anjos. I keep telling her, "I'm going to get back at you for pulling that one on me!"

My parents grew up so poor that when they immigrated to Canada, they saved every penny they earned to pass on to us kids. They never went on vacation or out to dinner or to a movie and never did anything fun. Their value system was to work hard and to sacrifice absolutely everything for the sake of their kids.

We had a family ritual. Every Sunday after church, my mother would make popcorn the old-fashioned way—with kernels and oil on the stove, and she would bag some cherries while my dad would grab his old camera and a blanket, and we'd all head to the local park. My brother and sisters and I would go talk to the old people in the park and feed the animals and birds. We would swim in the small toddler wading pool, which had a fountain in the middle. If I saw the man with a big chin (my bogeyman), I would hide underwater. This was the same park where he appeared to live and where I initially saw him. My sister Anjos would pull me up out of the water by my hair so that I wouldn't drown. Every once in a while on these Sunday outings, my dad would buy us ice cream. We didn't have a lot of money, but we still would have a good family time together. I fondly remember those times in the park because we genuinely liked each other and had fun just being out together as a family.

During the weekends while my mother worked at the factory, my sisters and I would thoroughly clean the house spick-and-span. We knew she liked the house to be very clean, and it was our way of showing her our love. We were excited to see her gleeful reaction to our efforts. We didn't often see her smile because she was always so tired. Later, as a young adult, I learned that every weekend is NOT spring cleaning. My mother sometimes showed her appreciation by making a special beef dinner with gravy even though it was not in her budget. She knew how much we loved and devoured it.

Despite our poverty and hardships, I have very fond and happy memories of my childhood. There was always someone to play with. Mealtimes were like an Indian-tribe gathering. We would sit on the floor with my mother in the middle as the Indian chief and her tribe around her. She would feed us one at a time and, in so doing, would look straight into our eyes with love and endearment.

When we would get home from school, we had to change out of our school clothes and into our playclothes or our PJs. Growing up, we were taught to take care of our things, and that included our clothes.

This made the clothes last longer. My twin sister, Anjos, and I were the lucky ones to get to wear the secondhand clothes first. Needless to say, I had a sheltered childhood. I remember a little girl on our street who was from a divorced family. She had all the toys I wished I had. I would spend most of my time there, mostly to play with her Barbie dolls and all her toys and to escape the reality of my poor and deprived life. She had more toys and clothes than all five of us kids. Reflecting back, I know that I was the rich kid because I had the love of my intact family. I learned the difference between the material world and the rich world of a loving family.

At Christmas time, I remember going with my father to a big building, which was probably a food bank. We would come back with sugar, a turkey, and prepackaged red fishnet Christmas stockings for all of us. I thought it was a palace because it was huge, with all kinds of goodies. I also remember getting the "mouse trap" game one Christmas, but the pieces looked like they had been chewed up by a dog. Clearly it was secondhand, but I played happily with it so many times. I suspect our toys were bought from the Salvation Army or a secondhand store of some kind. In our family, we did not hang Christmas stockings. But as kids, we didn't care. There were still toys to play with, and we were grateful for what we had. Our parents taught us an old Portuguese tradition of leaving our shoes on the stove on Christmas Eve so that they could be filled with gifts by morning.

All of us kids slept in the same bed, with my brother at the foot of the bed. I remember waking up from a nightmare one night and thinking that there was a green Martian in the bed, but it was just my brother's head.

At age eight, in grade four, I was told by my teacher that it appeared to him that I could not see very well. My teacher suspected that I was struggling to see the chalkboard and informed my parents of his suspicion. So my father took me for an eye test, and I got my first pair of glasses. I remember leaving the optometrist's office with my new glasses and looking up at the trees and seeing the leaves for the first time in my life. Before that, they were just a blur of green to me. I started to really see the world for the first time! I so appreciated seeing clearly, and pardon the pun, I never looked back!

At age thirteen, in junior high, I became aware of how I dressed in comparison to the other girls. I decided to get a part-time job. With my mother's help, I got a job at a clothing/textiles store in Kensington Market. It paid me twenty dollars a day for each Saturday I worked. Also, in our neighborhood, there was a trendy clothing store that sold current-style clothes at really low prices. One of the stores was Honest

Ed's. This allowed me to keep up with the styles without costing me too much. Dressing more like the others boosted my self-esteem and made me feel that I fit in better and was ready for high school.

High school was my universe. I worked very hard, and in my first semester, I made the honor roll. My parents were so proud of me because they never got a chance to go to high school. In fact, they only reached grade four in Portugal. I decided to set a goal to make the honor roll every semester for all four years, and I achieved this. My confidence level really heightened, and I was one of the popular "good girls." I achieved this while still helping out at home and working part-time. All subjects didn't come naturally to me, so I had to work my buns off. But I did it. I achieved an honors diploma, which, when I could afford it, I had it framed. To this day, my sisters are mad at me because since they followed me in school, they had many of the same teachers who compared them to me, and they hated that.

When I turned sixteen, my father wanted me to take driving lessons because I kept bringing up the fact that we were the only family without a car. He could not drive, of course, because he was completely blind in his right eye, and my mother was simply a nervous wreck. He paid for the driving lessons, and when I got my license, my father took out his savings and bought a car. It was a butter-colored Chevy Malibu.

Hurry Up and Slow Down—Laura's Story

I became the family's designated driver. I had to get up at 5:00 a.m. every morning to drive my mother and father to work. Then I walked to high school since it was just down the street. Slowly, over a long period of time, I felt that our family started to blend in with the other families. I thought about this because I never felt good about being poor or different. Hey, I was a teenager! What did I really know about the scheme of life?

Laura—Teenager

Also at age sixteen, I landed the best part-time job ever! I was the president of a fan club for a band called Edward Bear. I would work in the summer and part-time after school. My alias was Jennifer Green, and I would personally respond to all the fan mail that came in. The band practiced their music in a studio downstairs, and I could feel the floor vibrate from the electric guitars. The job was so cool, interesting, and fun. They recognized my good work, and soon, I became their booking agent. Even years later, they would send me their latest records as they were released. I absolutely loved that job, and it taught me a lot. Most people have to work for a living, so work at something you enjoy doing. If you are not happy with your job right now, do something about it! What are you waiting for?

My memories of my mother are that she was five-foot nothing in height, yet the strongest woman I have ever known. I have always had the utmost respect for her. She had an incredible inner strength, I thought, until we witnessed one of her panic attacks. It was the first time I saw her vulnerability. It happened on the day our dad was rushed to the hospital. My father, while on the job as a construction worker, fell on the ice and hit his head very hard. We got a call that he had an accident, had sustained a head injury, and had been rushed to the hospital. At the time, we had a married Portuguese couple renting upstairs. They spoke English, and they helped my mother and I get to the hospital in

Mississauga, where my father had been taken. We traveled by public transit. That was when we were told he had a brain tumor. He was only forty-four years young! It was a very long way by bus, so we were not able to visit him every day. He was actually slowly going blind but had not told anyone. Thanks to that accident, a CT scan was ordered and revealed the tumor. I was only twelve years old at the time. I felt that my life was shattered. But my mom needed help and someone to lean on, so I did whatever I could to support her. At that moment in time, we hugged each other and cried because we were so scared. My mother did not speak English, so I had to translate for her. My father needed surgery to remove the tumor. He was transferred to Toronto Western Hospital where Dr. Fleming operated on him. I remember praying for him every day before I went to school. The doctors were successful at removing most of the tumor, but there was damage to his optic nerve, and as a result, he went blind in his right eye. This was one of my first lessons on how precious life is and how it can change without notice.

Funny about associations—when I got home, Elton John's "Daniel" was playing on the radio, and to this day, it still reminds me of hope. Whenever I hear that song, these memories come back to haunt me. I learned a lot through this experience—how to give direction and take charge. I had to direct my mother to the hospital because she had a terrible sense of direction. She needed me to read the signs and speak

English for her to the hospital staff. I thought the worst that could happen was that my dad would die. Daily I prayed for the best. Even as a kid, I learned to condition my expectations and manage whatever came my way, thus developing coping strategies that I still apply today. What helped me deal with stuff was to mentally prepare for the worst-case scenario, and that way, I could deal with whatever came up. As young as I was, I thought my father was going to die, but luckily, he survived. As a kid, I would say my dad was still alive, and we'd pray for him to come home soon. My dad did come home but with impaired vision. I shifted my focus. I chose to become his eyes.

Luckily, the tumor was benign, but it grew back ten years later, and he had to have the same surgery again. Because of his illness, he could no longer work in the construction business. He got a new job as a dishwasher at a posh hotel in downtown Toronto. With his impaired vision, he had a tendency to break a lot of dishes and subsequently lost his job because of it. Throughout this time, my mother kept working and busting her buns to support my father and five kids. Over time, my father started showing signs of Alzheimer's but was never diagnosed of having it. However, he was diagnosed with having excess brain fluid that accumulated from the brain surgeries. It was highly recommended that he have a shunt put into his head to drain the fluid into his stomach. This was supposed to be a simple operation, but he fell into a coma. He remained in a vegetative state for four months. We visited him and prayed for him daily until his heart just gave out one day, and he died. I got the news at work and rushed to the hospital, crying like I had never cried before. I should not have even been driving, and I did not even make it in time before he passed away.

He was only sixty-four and didn't even get a chance to enjoy any retirement time. Thinking back, I should have taken time off from work to be with him. Hindsight is twenty-twenty. It's too bad we don't see so clearly in the present.

If you are in the retirement-eligibility window, what are you waiting for? If you are facing difficult times, stop and think. Set a plan as to how you may best handle the situation. Don't fly by the seat of your pants because you'll just get kicked in the ass.

When I was eighteen, I landed a job with a major international IT company where I worked for thirty-three years, and within that time period, I worked through eight different careers, including administration, business operations, marketing, education and training, business processes and reengineering, and human resources. These career paths spanned many jobs, which meant a new job every other year with some management positions. I always thrived on change and welcomed challenges.

Hurry Up and Slow Down—Laura's Story

Joe & Laura—High School Sweethearts

When I was nineteen, I married Joe, my high school sweetheart. This was when I learned about true romantic love. Joe was my first and only true love. Joe did the honorable and traditional thing by asking my father's permission to marry me before proposing.

Laura & Joe Wedding Pic

Both of us saved everything we made for our wedding. It was a hell of a party. Everyone said it was the most fun wedding they had ever been to. Seven years later, we had our first child, Jason. I couldn't balance work and raising Jason, and unfortunately, I put more time and energy into my work and not in being a mother. I deeply regret this, but at age thirty-five, when we had our second son, James, I still had not yet truly learned, and I continued to put as many hours into my work as I had with the first. Work-life balance in large companies is simply lip service and is not real or possible.

Laura's Mom

When my mother turned sixty-five, she retired and started to collect her government pension. She was a widow and very lonely. We asked her to move in with us and help with our second child. My mother always loved babies, and it brought out the kinder, sweeter side of her personality. When she lived with us, we included her in absolutely everything we did. When we went out to dinner or with friends, she came with us. We took her to the movies, the circus, the Ontario Place, the Toronto Zoo, and to restaurants, and she loved it. I remember and laugh about the first night she moved in, and we went out to dinner. On her first time eating out with us, she had seafood pasta and was so excited that she ate the shrimp tails. Mom always said someone else's cooking is always more enjoyable. It made me so happy to see her enjoying life and experiencing some things for the very first time, such as having birthday parties in her honor. I believe that if you have someone in your life who is not as privileged as you, help them to appreciate the better things in life. It will give you gratification to see the joy you bring to their lives.

Regrettably and unconsciously, I took advantage of the situation because James was home with his grandmother. I assumed that everything was fine. In reality, my mother was exhausted. James was the definition of a very active child, and he wore her out. My lesson learned is that just because you have a convenient arrangement for your family, this does not give you an excuse to spend more time working and believing everything will be OK. We all know and experience how time can just slip by us, and man, kids grow up way too fast. I learned this the hard way, so take stock of how you are spending your time. You may want to make some adjustments because you can't make more time or get it back. So what are you waiting for?

Laura & Joe—Happily Married

In 2012, Joe and I will be celebrating our thirty-fourth wedding anniversary. It hasn't always been bliss, but we've learned a lot and are still very much in love. More importantly, we really like each other as people. We're like best friends—most of the time, anyway.

What I learned is that the foundation of a strong and happy marriage is based on five pillars:

1. Genuine and undying love for each other
2. A strong commitment to each other
3. Working through challenges with the intent of staying in the marriage

4. Open and honest communication
5. Keeping the romance alive by continuing to date each other

I think all too often, couples give up too soon and walk away from their marriage.

Joe has so many of the same qualities that my father had, which is why I think I fell in love with him. I also believe meeting the right person can be based on destiny or just plain luck. Take the time to get to really know each other and live together because that's when you will really learn about each other.

I had a miscarriage the year before Jason was born; needless to say, Jason was a huge extra-special blessing to both of us. Joe was working shifts then, so most of the time, it was just Jason and I. In retrospect, I babied him too much because as a toddler, he became a mama's boy. I even remember him crying for me when I went out one evening and left him home with Joe. I had to make adjustments in my role as a mom.

Jason has grown up to be a fine young man and quite the scholar. He achieved his master's degree in philosophy at the ripe age of twenty-four. I'd like to think he inherited his thirst for learning from me and a strong work ethic from the Portuguese bloodline. Jason is now in his chosen career in the academic field.

James is seventeen and in his final year of high school. He has made the honor roll for two consecutive years for grades ten and eleven. This

is especially significant considering the stresses at home and his extra responsibilities (which I will speak of later). So this is particularly amazing in my mind. Even with all the challenges at home, James still managed to attain these achievements. I am so proud of him, and I tell him every day how he is growing up to be a fine young man.

I believe a mother's job is to teach her sons to be good husbands, and a father's job is to teach them to become good dads. James recently got his G2 driver's license and is now attending college for a co-op apprenticeship program to be an electrician. That's great because in Canada, there is a huge need for tradespeople. Can you tell I'm just bursting at the seams with pride for our sons?

My near-death experience has prompted me to write this story as a form of therapy for myself and for the benefit of others who may go through what I have gone through these past eighteen months.

During my recovery, James was so helpful. He would help Joe with some of the household duties and would help me find the earrings I wanted to wear and set out my clothes the night before like I used to do for him when he was a child. Talk about role reversal! Jason would also come home on weekends to help out even though he had a full-time job and a busy social schedule.

James always makes it a point to come see me to say good-bye and kiss me before he leaves for school. I always said "Have a nice day," but recently changed it to "Make it a great day."

My mother suffered a stroke at age seventy-six. Unfortunately, she didn't receive any physiotherapy, so she was left incapacitated. She is in a wheelchair and in a nursing home. Ironically, she is back in the area where she raised her family in a nursing home called Kensington Gardens. Fortunately, she met her guardian angel, a PSW (personal support worker) called simply K. I have often seen them together, and they genuinely love and care for each other. I know my mother is getting the best care with K, and this gives me peace of mind. It is as if destiny had laid this out. I visit her as often as I can, but sadly, she does not recognize me or any of her children anymore. She has dementia, which is of course part of the effects of her stroke. She is now eighty-two years young. She is content, but it breaks my heart that she has lost her faculties and memories. My mother is still in Kensington Gardens, and thankfully, K still works there.

Joe had been working at a major Canadian car manufacturing company and, in 2009, had decided to take an early retirement after thirty-three years of service. Once retired, he would walk me to the front door as I would leave for the office, give me a kiss, and wave me out the door and, all the while, asking me when I might be retiring. Joe has two very passionate hobbies: raising and racing pigeons and fishing. Those keep him very active and happy. I think everyone should have a hobby. I have tried to take up hobbies, but I just never found the time or the right one for me, although I've always been an avid reader, but that's not a hobby. The lesson I learned is that you have to create the time, not try to find the time. People who have hobbies live longer and happier lives, so I am exploring new ideas.

As a kid, I never had a real Barbie doll—you know, the one whose arms and legs really bend. Many years later, I acquired a desire to have one of my very own. When I turned forty, Joe put up a surprise birthday party for me. Our son Jason gave me a real Barbie doll as his gift. He knew my story, of course, and he got me the clothes and everything. I was very touched by that sweet and thoughtful gift, and I played with Barbie all day. It was one of the sweetest and thoughtful things Jason ever did for me. Over the years, I got my sisters' Barbies as well, and when we get together, just for fun, we'd play with them.

After some financial planning, I decided to take an early retirement effective July 1, 2010, in what I now call the summer from hell. During the first two weeks of July, we took a vacation and stayed at a cottage. I had my sister Mary Jo come with us, as she had in previous years. We were having a great time. Mary Jo and Joe had gone fishing and caught some fish. That Tuesday, July 13, 2010, was the most horrifying day that I will never forget. Joe and I were awakened very early by screams for help. I was in a daze but recognized that it was Mary Jo's voice. Joe and I followed her voice and ran outside to find her flat on her back and unable to move. She was in excruciating back pain. I tickled her foot, and she felt nothing, and she didn't move or twitch. She was unable to remember how she got on the ground on her back. We called 911 and got her to the closest hospital, which was in North Bay, Ontario. They ran some initial tests and arranged to have her transferred to Toronto Western Hospital. I accompanied her on a small plane. It reminded me of *The Amazing Race*, but in this case, it was to save a life. We landed at Toronto Island Airport then took the ferry across to the dock, onto an ambulance, and from there, to the hospital. This all took seven hours. All the while, I was having panic attacks because I was so worried about Mary Jo. I could only think of the impact this accident would have on Mary Jo's life.

That night, she underwent back surgery. Mary Jo had shattered a couple of vertebrae and had broken two ribs. She had also severed her spinal cord. My worst fears came to fruition—she became paralyzed from the waist down at the age of forty-nine. My brother and sisters and I rallied around her because she was alone in life. As a family, we promised to do anything and everything to help her. I visited her every day at the hospital. Mary Jo was later transferred to Toronto Rehab Spinal Cord Injury Center, called Lyndhurst Centre. I continued to visit her every day and made her her favorite tuna-fish sandwiches. Every day we'd eat lunch together, and then we'd go outside for some fresh air. I had to put on my happy face, smile, and make her laugh. Learning to live without the use of her legs has been the most difficult period of adjustment. She was also single as she had lost her life partner in an accident a few years prior to her own accident. Mary Jo was always so happy-go-lucky. All that changed in the blink of an eye.

Since the accident, Mary Jo had to sell her house because modifying it would have been too costly. She moved into a wheelchair-accessible apartment in downtown Toronto. The complex provides medical assistance. She cooks her own meals and looks after herself as best she can. She made the best of a very bad and challenging situation.

The following month, during the evening of August 29, 2010, while at home with Joe, I received a phone call with bad news. Suddenly, I experienced a violent headache that felt like an explosion went off in my head and lost consciousness. I later learned that I had suffered from a ruptured brain aneurysm that caused a stroke. I was only fifty-one. I complained of a massive headache. Fortunately, my family got me to Toronto Western Hospital relatively quick, and I was operated on to clip the ruptured blood vessel. This left me paralyzed on my left side (I wasn't able to move it at all). I also lost my left peripheral vision, which the medical profession calls left-side neglect. By the time I got to Toronto Western Hospital, I was in a coma. The doctors told Joe and our sons that I was more dead than alive.

The neurosurgeon who saved my life was Dr. Christopher Wallace. He worked with Dr. Fleming, who was the surgeon who operated on my father. Talk about full circle! I later learned that Dr. Fleming retired many years ago.

While I was an inpatient at Toronto Western Hospital for two months, I had some of my darkest moments. I was hopeful my menopause had stopped because I no longer had hot flashes. I was also wondering what kind of life I would have and how it would affect me and my family. I found it very difficult to remember nurses' names. This was important to me because I believe everyone wants to be called by their name. Everyone, from your grocery store cashier to anyone else you encounter in your daily life, wants to be called by his/her name.

To keep my mind active, I made it a point to remember all of the nurses' names. Since I was only a few weeks into retirement, my mind was still in business mode and had not yet decluttered my thinking. In my head, I started to develop a business plan of how I would run this hospital if I were the operating director. I set this as my goal even though I was uncertain of the future or how much control I would have. These by far were some of my darkest days—I did not like the nurses at this hospital, I had no TV in my room, and I was very bored.

I got some physical healing while at Toronto Western Hospital. I vowed that I would do whatever I could for a complete and full recovery, no matter how long it would take. But then I felt like I was not focusing on the right things. I shifted my focus to myself and tried to wiggle my fingers and toes or move my leg or arm. Nothing! No movement! I was scared to death! So I started to focus on my body. My recovery would be my new job. Talk about getting my priorities straight! I envisioned this road to recovery with Joe, Jason, Jamie, and Shadow, our beautiful golden retriever. At the end of this road, I also envisioned that I would be with my precious husband and children and all my friends and the rest of my family cheering me on at the roadsides. It was during this time that I took stock of my life and decided that I would make some different choices, given the circumstances. For example, I stopped wearing my watch because time didn't matter. One day, take off your watch and see how it makes you feel. I bet you'll feel much more relaxed and carefree and not living minute to minute. For me, it was like time no longer existed.

What a catastrophic change in my life, to go from a strong self-sufficient woman to a helpless being. What a blow to my self-esteem and whole being! I would often make a parallel comparison to a toddler—making the transition from wearing a diaper to toilet training to learning to feed herself and getting dressed with help and relearning how to stand

and to walk. It had been, and still is, a lot of hard work with lots of terrible pain. This time, I was fighting for my life. It was so difficult to go from being a fast-paced woman who worked eighteen hours a day on most days and ran a household with only two hours of sleep a night to a woman who lies in a hospital bed all day.

I set a major goal for myself—I wanted my life back. I vowed I would have a full and complete recovery, no matter how long it would take. Nobody could give me a prognosis because every case was different. There were no given timelines in these situations. This illness was a major tragedy for me and my family. Despite this catastrophic disaster in my life, I consider myself very lucky in so many ways:

- I am lucky to be alive.
- I am lucky to have the opportunity, to some degree, to be able to live some of my life over again.
- I am lucky to be able to truly appreciate my family and friends better.
- I am lucky to be able to make changes in my life and set better priorities.
- I am lucky to be able to appreciate better the true meaning of life and happiness.

- I am lucky to have and appreciate better my relationship with my loving husband and great sons who continue to support and help me through this, the most difficult time of my life.
- I am lucky to have my mind and cognitive skills intact.
- I am lucky to have maintained a sense of humor and the ability to laugh and smile.

When I needed help in the hospital, I would call the nurse by name. Every morning, I would vow that I would make someone laugh that day, and I would laugh with them. I love to laugh, and I really believe that "laughter is the best medicine." Whenever I read *Reader's Digest*, their "Laughter Is the Best Medicine" is what I always read first. I love a good belly laugh—you know, the one that makes you bend over because it makes you feel so good. I have always incorporated humor in my everyday life.

From Toronto Western Hospital, I was later transferred to Toronto Rehabilitation Institute (TRI) Neuro/Stroke Centre on University Avenue, Toronto. I was an inpatient there for three months in their neuro center for acquired brain-injury patients. I underwent extensive rehabilitation to try to recover some mobility on my left side. While I was there, I learned a new f-word. That word is FOCUS. I had to stop myself and say aloud, "Focus, Laura."

Joe visited me every day, and sometimes, he would make and bring me my favorite lunch—tuna-fish sandwiches. He'd bring a bottle of Tabasco sauce along with salt-and-vinegar chips and Diet Coke. We would eat together, and I would be in my glory. Every Sunday, he and our sons would come to spend the day with me. I lived for these Sundays to see and spend time with them. One Sunday in late October 2010, James, who is very calm and cool as a cucumber, stood by my bedside, looked at me straight in the eye, and said, "Mom, you know, these days I have been thinking a lot about my blessings and what I am most grateful for."

I said, "Tell me, James, what are you most grateful for?"

He responded, "For you, Mom—that you are alive, and that I have you."

Tears of joy ran down my face. I asked him to write his thoughts in a letter for me so I could put it in my treasure box and have it always to read again and again. So you see, teenagers can have feelings too! If you have teenage children, be open with your affection for them, and they will reciprocate. It might be awkward at first, but they will always come through. James also told me that our dog, Shadow, a beautiful golden lab retriever, had been waiting at our front door the entire time I was in the hospital, just waiting for me to come home.

I learned to move and lift my left leg and arm to some degree. I was able to lift my leg and move my hand after considerable therapy. I learned that patience is more than just a virtue; it's reality when life bites you in the ass. With my type of injury, recovery is very, very slow. These were, by far, very tough times for me because the therapy was extremely intense, and I would experience severe chronic and excruciating pains. I was so weak that I could not even turn in bed by myself. One night, after the nurse had gotten me ready for bed and I was in a nice sleep, I woke up trying to turn to my right side, and that in itself was torture. I did a teeter-totter motion, rocking back and forth, trying to turn over to my right side. I was always being put to bed on my back, but I am a belly sleeper, so you can imagine my anguish. Of course, the sheets were all getting tangled up throughout this process. When I woke up from my nightmare, I felt like there was an octopus pulling me down to the bottom of the ocean, and I started to scream for help. Awake, I realized I was tangled up in the sheets—that was the "octopus" in my bed. This was when I started to learn to see the humor in things and laughed out loud by myself. I am sure the nurses laughed later in the staff room at me, but that's OK. It was funny, and it's OK to laugh at yourself because it just makes you more human. It was during this time that I discovered I was actually pretty funny. All my family and friends commented that I had changed in that way, and it cracked them up. I think it was due to the combination of losing my social filter and being able to recognize the funny side of situations more easily.

I was also an outpatient at Toronto Rehabilitation Rumsey Centre for six months. With the help and encouragement from Joe and our sons, I continued to work hard on physiotherapy at home. I taught myself some hand tricks just to keep my fingers in motion, and I entertain my friends with those and some select hand gestures. I could now walk using a quad cane. I was released and came home for Christmas 2010. My hard work and focus were paying off. I attribute the success of my recovery to the following: sheer determination and hard work, realistic expectations and a big dose of patience, taking things day by day, a positive "can do" attitude, and the love and support of my family and all my great friends.

Because of my vision loss, I couldn't drive anymore, and Joe had to chauffeur me to all my appointments. We called myself Miss Daisy. One day while driving to physiotherapy, I said, "People say I am so funny now. Maybe I'll be a stand-up comedian."

Joe's reply was, "That's fine but you can't stand." So I answered, "Then I'll be a sit-down comedian."

Shortly after I started with Toronto Rehab at the Rumsey Centre as an outpatient, I set specific, clear-cut goals for myself. Getting more mobile more quickly was my most important and highest priority. I remember sitting in the family room with Joe one Sunday afternoon shortly after starting my physiotherapy. I said, "Joe, I want to walk."

He said, "OK" and took my arm, and I walked on my own two feet for the first time since August 2010. It just goes to show that with the right positive mind-set and by setting goals and sheer determination and intense focusing, one can achieve anything one wants. Rumsey became almost my second home because I would go there almost every other day. The drive was almost fifty kilometers each way. Joe graciously offered and had been driving me like Miss Daisy ever since. But Joe hated traffic and would get so frustrated with the long drive downtown. We had to have a few time-outs with him. Joe learned a new f-word too. His f-word was *frustrated*. If there was a Husband of the Year award, Joe would definitely be the recipient.

On one of our drives to the Rumsey Centre, I told Joe I was experiencing chest pains and having difficulty breathing. Upon arriving at the center, we went directly across the street to the cardio center. There, an older female cardiologist saw me and asked a few questions. I was surprised she didn't listen to my chest. Instead, she had a technician do an ECG on me. The results indicated that it was not a cardiac arrest. WHEW! What a relief! I was a bit hesitant but told the doctor, "This morning, I put on a brand-new underwire bra, and it is very uncomfortable. Do you suppose this has anything to do with what I am feeling?"

She said it might. So we removed my bra. LOL! I felt free as a bird! On the drive back home, I told Joe, "Thank God it wasn't a heart attack. It was just a bra attack!"

Dr. Wallace was checking my recovery one day, and sitting on his stool, he asked me to kick as high as I could. I suggested that he might want to back away, but he said he'd take his chances. There I was, joking around with a brain surgeon. Prior to my injury, I don't think I could have done that, but we had a great laugh together, and he did not sustain any injuries.

I am now able to better appreciate all the wonderful friends that I have. Most notable is my dearest best friend, Dianne Richards, whom I met initially at work some thirty years ago. Most of my friendships were initiated through work, and I have and will continue to maintain them over many years. While I was in the hospital, Dianne set up a blog for me on a website called Care Pages. Care Pages is a website that allows updates of a patient's progress, and it gave my friends an opportunity to post their messages for me as well. My friends' messages described me as an inspiration, and this motivated me to live up to that perception. I read words that one generally only hears at funerals, and the recipient isn't there to enjoy them. I learned that it is important to make time for your friends, and if you share your heart, they will reciprocate. I learned how Dianne felt about me through this process and how she would often say "I will kill you if you die!" Dianne is the best friend anyone could ever hope to have. She would always offer and do anything I needed her to do, such as taking me to the hospital when I had a miscarriage and picking up Jason from day care when I was running late from work. We call her Auntie Di.

While I was in the hospital, one of my biggest fears was to fall back into a coma, so I decided to write letters to the three men in my life—Joe, James, and Jason. I did it as if I was speaking with my last breath. It might sound a little morbid, but I just wanted to be sure that I wouldn't miss the opportunity to express my deepest feelings. I wanted them to know how much I loved them and how I could not have survived without their love and support.

After three months, I came home on a day pass and got so much loving from Shadow. She spoke to me in her little doggie language and said, "Where the heck have you been? I love you, Mom! I've missed you!

Now come over here and give me a pat and a hug!" She has not left my side since. She seems to worry that when I go out, I may not come back and would wait again at the door for my return, greeting me warmly each time. Man, she sure can wag her tail ferociously.

After I came home, I occasionally had a feeling that someone would put a hand on my left shoulder. I like to believe it was my dad as my guardian angel. Joe told me I was crazy. I had this feeling quite often, but then one day, I noticed that my bra strap had slipped down my shoulder because of my shoulder muscle loss. So I discovered that it was not my guardian angel but my bra strap. Damn the bras!

Toronto Western Hospital has a partnership with the Toronto Rehabilitation Institute. Since I had such tremendously positive experiences with TRI, during one of my checkups with Dr. Wallace, I shared my experiences with him and said I would be happy to be involved with their marketing and advertising. Dr. Wallace said, "You could be their next poster babe." That put a huge smile on my face.

Another dear friend of mine, Jenny O' Brien, gave me an aha moment while having dinner with her at TRI. Every Monday, she'd bring me dinner, and we'd share that meal together, and we'd talk and laugh for hours. One day, I was having a pity party. I was feeling sorry for myself and wondering why this happened to me, a good person, when there are bad people and criminals in jail. She hugged me and said, "Lala [my nickname], I love you, and you are an amazing lady. I am glad you are alive, and you are going to be fine. You will teach us all by writing the book you have always wanted to write."

I believe things happen for a reason. This inspired me to write and share my experiences. Now I get it—I understand why this has happened to me. It was a rough thing to go through just to have material for a book.

What I have learned from this difficult time is the meaning of true love and commitment. Joe has remained by my side through the roughest period of our marriage. Joe's commitment to our marriage, to help me through this, has been vital to my recovery. He was my pillar of strength. He made big sacrifices through unselfish efforts that he went through to help me, and it was a commitment and labor of love. I learned how much I mean to my son James when he told me how he feared he'd lose me and how much I mean to him. He counted his blessings that I was still alive. I learned to have more discussions with my sons, you know, even the touchy-feely ones they don't like. I also learned that the meaning of real, true friendships is when your friends come over to make a meal and enjoy it with your family and other friends, like Diane Beard who took time from her personal life to come over and type this book for me as I couldn't type anymore. What a blow to my ego to go from 110 WPM to hunting and pecking with my right index finger. Thank you, Diane.

Most of all, I learned the true value of life and how very precious and fragile life is and how, in the blink of an eye, it can all change. I took good care of myself, ate well, and exercised regularly, so I was not prepared for this catastrophe. This could happen to anyone, even you. So take stock of your life now while you can and make sure your focus is on the things that are most important to you.

I learned how smart and genuinely good my husband and sons are, and I should have praised them more often long ago. Just the other day, I said to Joe, "Man, you are handsome." I should have said that more often. I said, "You have beautiful eyes." He responded, "That's what they all say." "Who says?" I asked, and Joe replied, "You know, all the ladies."

Recently, Fred, a good friend of mine, told me I have a beautiful soul that shines like a light to inspire others. This was a lovely comment that made me feel good. This reminded me that we must tell the people who are important in our lives what they mean to us while we have the opportunity, rather than at their funeral or memorial service, where they won't hear it anymore.

I always thought I was reasonably good-looking, but everyone told me, once I got out of the hospital, that I looked beautiful. I wondered what had changed. There is truth in the saying that beauty comes from within. I realized that I was at peace, probably from coming so close to death and a life-altering event. My niece's husband said I even looked younger. I thought I knew what stress was when I was working and stuck in the rat race, but not until this had happened to me did I learn that stress is not living life to its fullest. I learned that we take far too much for granted. Try going to the washroom and dressing yourself with one hand, especially if you are wearing jeans or pants. Then try tying a shoelace with one hand, and drying and styling your hair with one hand, or cutting up the food on your plate with one hand. These are some of the things we take for granted until we have to find a way to deal with a challenge. There is truth that beauty is from within. When I was in the hospital, they removed part of my skull to relieve the pressure from the swelling of my brain, so it was caved in, and I called myself pothead. When they shaved my head and put in the staples, I called myself zipper-head punk rocker. Everyone got to see all my gray hair, but I had my lipstick on. I was notoriously known for always having lipstick on, and I always had it on in the hospital too. I left my kiss stamp on a lot of cheeks, so you always know when Lala has been in the room. Humpty Dumpty got put back together again, and so was I. I had my bone flap on my forehead put back, my hair colored and highlighted again. That helped me look a lot better and feel better too!

We need to put things into perspective. My sister Mary Jo will never walk again. So next time you think you're having a bad day, stop, rethink, and remind yourself of the positive things in your life and think about Mary Jo. We need to learn to appreciate what we have before it's gone. We must be thankful for our abilities and, more importantly, for the people in our lives. Sounds cliché, but it is also true that the most important thing in life is your health. As a kid, my mother used to say that all the time, but I had no idea what she meant until I lost my good health. Now I have to teach this to my sons and to you, my readers.

Some really good things have come out of this experience for me. It started with removing myself from the rat race, taking a deep breath, and being grateful every day that I am alive. I wake up wondering how I can make someone else happy today. I count my blessings and appreciate what I have and don't take it for granted anymore. My mind and my recovery progress are far more important than money or possessions. My personality has changed, bringing out the better parts of me—humility, sense of humor, true appreciation, and the softer, sweeter side. The intensity within me disappeared along with the sense of urgency, and my sweeter side came out, which certainly helped my relationships, especially with Joe and my sons. That's easier to do when you are not being sucked by a demanding job, and my recovery became my new job just like when I was still a career woman. Focus, determination, and hard work are helping me survive and live on.

I started a day program as part of my recovery and to be among people who have also been through brain injury—some from car accidents, some from brain aneurysms, and some from strokes. I met one man, age twenty-five, who had a brain injury through aneurysm at age twelve. He was one the most intelligent people I have ever met. He looked like Johnny Depp, and we played games and had an event each week. We played boccie, and I learned to like it. When I joined it, I decided to say "Happy Monday," and it made everyone smile, and now they say to me, "Happy Monday." If you smile at people and say something different, like "Happy Monday," they will smile back. I have a new motto, and you might want to try it out. When I finish a communication, whether it is an e-mail, a telephone call, or a visit, I say three things: "Take care of yourself," "Keep smiling," and "Be happy," and I live by that!

As for me, it has been just over a year since my aneurysm and stroke, and I am walking with a quad cane and will be retiring my wheelchair soon. I still have little use of my left arm and hand but can do some unique hand gestures for entertainment. An unusual thing—my memory improved through all this when most lost theirs.

Recently, I achieved a new milestone. I am now walking 150 meters with my quad cane, and soon, I will join a marathon—well, maybe—or at least chase Joe around the house. The best part will be when I catch him.

Having been at death's door, I have reflected much about my life and how I have lived it. At some point or another, we all have regrets in our lives. When I was still working, I was your typical personality: type A, doing ten things at a time for work and personal life. I was always in a hurry, dropping some balls every once and a while. Having this stroke forced me to slow down. It won't be easy to change the things in your life that you are not happy with and stop putting things off that are important to you and will make you happy. There are enough miserable people on this earth; don't add to the heap. When you are happy, you will make those around you happy.

I have enriched my friendships by being more humble and by finally writing my story and by mentally taking care of myself. I was too serious and intense previously, and now, I really focus on the humor in things. I have appreciated the smaller things in life, like a nice cup of tea or a glass of wine.

When it comes to regrets, I am no different, but I decided to do something about those regrets so that I would not take them to my grave. Many years ago, I had an unresolved altercation with Jason, and I recently made peace with him. Tim McGraw's song "Live Like You Were Dying" had really resonated with me. I decided to title my book *Hurry up and Slow Down*. Don't let illness or misfortune force you to slow down; make a conscious effort to focus on what is important in life and start now. So HURRY UP AND SLOW DOWN. Take control of your life now while you can. Slow down and enjoy life.

Acknowledgements

My first thanks goes to the men in my life. I thank Joe and for his undying love and commitment, and to our two sons, James and Jason. A heartfelt thanks to James because he carried the burden by helping out at home on a daily basis and giving Joe some breaks. It gave me a chance to reconnect with James's tender heart. Thanks to my older son, Jason, who often comes home on weekends to pitch in, giving Joe and Jamie a break. This difficult time, I feel, has brought me closer to my sons.

Dr. Christopher Wallace saved my life, and for a brain surgeon, he is a really nice guy with a sense of humor. The first time I met him while conscious was three months after my surgery, and I said to him, "So you are the man who was in my head." I am eternally grateful for his skills and compassion. I had this image of him before I met him, or what I thought a neurosurgeon would look like. I thought he would be tall and slender and wearing hospital gear, but instead, he looked like a business executive, quite handsome and charming, and he appreciated my sense of humor. We clicked immediately. He had wonderful bedside manner. He had the ability to immediately put you at ease and spoke plain English instead of medical mumbo jumbo, and we immediately established a strong rapport. It's always good to have that with a medical specialist.

I want to acknowledge and thank all the wonderful people from Toronto Rehab Institute, namely my physiotherapists Irene, Fariba, Vivian, and Jeremy.

I want to thank my occupational therapists Heidi, Jack, Parvin, and Christine. I think I am one of their success stories, and I have told them I would be their next commercial spokesperson. I thank all of them for their caring dedication.

I want to give a huge thanks to all my wonderful friends who have supported and encouraged me every step of the way (pun intended). They called me inspirational and admired me for what I have accomplished. I never thought of myself as an inspiration, but if I can help others from my experiences, I thought a book could reach many people. I am working damn hard on my recovery. There is paralysis with a stroke, but there is also a lot of pain. My friends have really impacted me and my recovery. A big shout-out of thanks to Dianne and Warren, Leslie and Austin, Lucy and Mike, Wendy Pooh and Greg, Karen and Randy, Sue and Randy, Linda and Dino, Little Linda, Ed and Miss Bessy, Monica, Pat and Sharon, Susan, Jenny O. and Jenny Tung, KK and Donna, Sharon H., Brenda and Tony, Lucy and Mike, Donna and Wes, Maria, Troy, Lisa, CD, Joan, Karen, Deborah, and Lisa P.

I'd like to say a huge thanks to my brother and sisters for their love and support. The lesson learned here is to appreciate your friends at every opportunity. Don't wait for a major event.

Every day, I keep my mind on my goal for a full and complete recovery, no matter how long it takes. I have worked very hard in my rehab despite the chronic and debilitating pain. By sheer determination and the strong work ethics that I learned from my parents, I persevered. And you can do this too in your life when you focus on your goals and aspirations.

I want to share with you one of my favorite quotes: "This is a year of appreciation and fulfillment. The more you appreciate everything is your life, the more fulfillment you'll have. Life loves to give to those who appreciate what they already have. Be giving to others. Life will be given to you. Feel blessed, and blessings will show upon you. Expect only good each day. Your thoughts and words do matter. Life is always responding to whatever you think and say. Harness the power of your words and you'll have dominion over your life and experiences" (Louise L. Hay).

We are all caught up in a rat race. We want bigger and better homes and better lives than we had for our children. A wise person told me once that "we work to live, not live to work." I should have followed that advice, but life should not be about "should haves" but about what we will—I will enjoy the smell of freshly cut grass, I will enjoy the sound of chirping birds, I will enjoy and have fun at this family reunion, and I will take care of myself so that I am alive to enjoy my grandchildren. I will be a better person for myself and my family. I will treat others the way I want to be treated. I will call people by name because people love to hear their name. My advice to you is to *hurry up and slow down!* Live life to the fullest because you never know when you might lose it.

Here are my life lessons that I would like to share with you:

- Hurry up and slow down.
- Focus on the really important things in life, which should be your family and friends, while creating happy times and memories, especially for your children.
- Never take things for granted, and live life to its fullest.
- Allow yourself to play and have fun (let your inner kid out to play).
- Laugh at yourself and say "It's OK, I am still learning."
- Be a positive role model.

- Deal with your regrets and move on.
- If you have baggage with someone, deal with it; forgive and it will release you.
- Hug and kiss your loved ones before you leave the house.
- Tell the people you love what and how much they mean to you, and do it regularly.
- There are no dress rehearsals in life, and it is OK to make mistakes as long as you learn from them and don't repeat them.
- Own up to the mistakes you do make.
- Make the best of your bad situations and learn from them.
- Set goals and plans to keep your focus on what you need or want to accomplish.
- Have a positive daily self-talk.
- Don't put off until tomorrow what you can do today.
- Smile, no matter what kind of day you are having. Smiling is contagious.
- Have a good belly laugh at least once a day. Laugh out loud (don't hold back).
- Treat others with respect and kindness (what goes around comes around).

I share with you my new mantra, which is "Hurry up and slow down."

Ferreira family on vacation in Sao Miguel, Azores, Portugal